A DIFFERENT PHYSICS

POEMS

LISA ROSENBERG

Abiding thanks to the editors of the following publications in which these poems appeared or are forthcoming, some in earlier versions.

The American Journal of Poetry: "Left Coast Triptych"
The Bitter Oleander: "Moon Jellies"
Bottomfish: "Blackboard"
Negative Capability: "Polygraph"
Nimrod: "Lessons," "Piece Parts"
Poetry magazine: "Archaeopteryx," "Attica," "Candle Lighting," "Introduction to Methods of Mathematical Physics," "Night Fire," "Woman from Fire"
Revolutionary Wellness Magazine: "Offering"
Shenandoah: "The Big White Dress"
Southwest Review: "To the Makers"
The Threepenny Review: "The Satellite Sky"
Witness: "Night," "Assembly," "Maze," "Laboratory"

"The Big White Dress" appears in the *Poetry Daily* anthology. "Introduction to Methods of Mathematical Physics" appears in *The POETRY Anthology: 1912–2002*, and online at *Intersections—Poetry with Mathematics*. The *Poetry Daily* website featured "Night," "Assembly," "Maze," "Laboratory," "The Big White Dress," and "Introduction to Methods of Mathematical Physics." "To the Makers" received the 2015 second place Morton Marr Prize. "Moon Jellies" won the 2003 Frances Locke Memorial Award. Several poems in this collection were publicly presented at the San Mateo County Board of Supervisors meetings, Redwood City, California, 2016-2018.

ISBN 978-0-9985140-6-2
Printed in the United States of America

RED MOUNTAIN PRESS

Santa Fe, New Mexico

www.redmountainpress.us

To my mentors,
present and ever-present

CONTENTS

III. MODELS

A DIFFERENT PHYSICS

INTRODUCTION TO METHODS OF MATHEMATICAL PHYSICS

You must develop a feeling for these symbols
that crawl across a page, for the text overrun

with scorpions. Like those books about insects
you read as a child, scared to touch the magnified photos,

this too will taunt you. It will become
your daily fare and meditation, your bedtime

reading, morning prayer. Soon a single Greek letter
makes your eyes smart. You find yourself flat

at the back of your skull, searching past daybreak
for the hidden path, the gilded key, a glimpse

of what those few must see at will, those few for whom
each equation is a playful catch, like bees into a jar.

I. A SKY RETOLD

PERSEVERANCE

Take back those keepers
of wonder—

The swan's back, brown creeper,
and golden grouse.

The flirty tails.
The talons, arched
like a map's edge.

I'm finished with plumage.

Etch me a classic, a girl
like Sisyphus, in pewter hues,

pushing
a corner of sky.

ATTICA

I expected something
oracular to come to me
there above the whitecaps
and gilded cliffs
at the tip of Attica.

It's what happens
in those landscapes.

Salt spray.
Autumn crocus.
The Temple of Poseidon
backlit by dusk
and I wanted

to come upon
the startled lizards
and wildflowers
without questions,

to turn and find

myself ready,
and the journey laid out.

360°

To bank over and turn around a point,
nothing but sky framing your high wing,
and fields below. Tree canopies, streams, sparse roads.
Both the shadow of a low cloud, and the cloud
whose flight path glides beneath your own.
A band of soft hills leading to the coast, the voice
of sun on the horizon's ageless arc.

SLIDE RULE

Tool of elegance,
of speed
against a different meter
of a different day:

a day you walked out to
suburbs and cars
and the faithful hold

of motor oil
on hot asphalt.
And orange blossoms.

A sky ripe
for the faint
drone of airplanes,

their hulls designed
with a lined precision
and the fortitude

of hand calculations.
Of penciled graphs.
Blueprints

and circle templates
on an angled
drafting board.

Mechanical tools
where mechanical
telephone bells

call through the plumes
above crowded
ashtrays and

coffee rings
on flecked Formica.
The desks

in rows, the men
in ties and shirtsleeves.
I am almost

there in my pixie cut
and white shoes
on Family Day.

Agape at the dark
control room.
Unaware of

the beauty
of logarithms,
the fluid promises

of computing.
That this laminate
rule will soon

outlast its heyday,
a burnished leather
case, and all of us.

There is war
on the news. We are
scaling the moon

and everyone
I love is living
or yet to be born.

BULL THISTLE

Pink crown on a globe of thorns on a stem of spines.
Smooth threads, like corn-silk, the burst top of choke
that stuns without a sound—sudden color
on a slow day, working its way outward.

Sentinel of the overgrown footpath.
Trader of sun, indifferent to sparse shelter
of bay laurel, eucalyptus, and madrone.

Scattered kin of artichoke, of wild stars
whose signature is borne across our skin.
We touch them, dry or just opened, nodding
with the weight of bees. Each fattened calyx

a promise of surprise when we open
to stories in the ungroomed underbrush,
to the sweet aftertaste of soft leaf-flesh.

HOUSE-SITTING

Sunshine for days now. The ersatz spring
has drugged me, keeps me pinned
to the porch of this house.

In a canvas chair I look up from my book:
temperate air, a slight breeze,
something of my grandparents' house

in the potted orange trees and red cement,
the pale yellow railing.
And the street's demeanor,

quiet except for birds, an occasional car.
A wall of camellias lined their yard,
a chain-link gate at the driveway.

Where are the giant magnolias
at the foot of the lawn, the planter box
in the picture? Shall I tell them

my aunt is dying, that it's only February
and everything's in bloom—
they are coming up the walk

dressed in cotton and plaid,
his cancer a decade away yet, her heart
humming on its clean new valve.

NIGHT FIRE

Over those hills
no one could walk:
those molten swells
that thread the dark.

Is it destruction we watch,
cathartic flame,
or a night city
viewed from a plane?

The amber-gilled
interior breathes soot
that rolls clear out
to where embers float

like porch-lit
suburbia, windows
warm with TV. Each fat
glow a homefire,

a trusted beacon
that won't be snuffed.
That shrill convergence
becomes downtown,

the flaring arms
of thoroughfares packed
with steamy hoods,
headlights fixing their cones

of white smoke,
the drivers unaware
of any tragedy, the grid
of streets warped

by some mysterious
heat. The city is
oblivious to pain.
It can't be reasoned with.

All night it flickers
the indifference
of office towers
and sleepless neon.

The street lamps hiss
their sodium.
This is normal for them.
They burn toward dawn,

they vanish where
the firestorm laid its
black path to greet us,
and moved on.

WOMAN FROM FIRE
after a sculpture by Rochelle Ford

Our Lady of Rebar, early with child,
her limbs culled from the Oakland fire,
curled by heat of sheetrock,
shingles, books, love letters, wire.
Her legs from white porticos.
One pipe-arm and a sprinkler eye
that watered lemon trees for years
when the knobs of her spine lay
hidden by mortar and siding,
until freed. Each bar chosen
from the ash, fitted, welded fast
to hold the smallest hard finding.

THE POPLAR

A poplar
by the evergreen forest
is a token,

its element
a different woodland,
not these

old groves and ancient forms:

needle, cone, and frond.
The flush of seedlings
after fire.
Impress of ferns.

Then a poplar
burning out of place

the autumn palette
of a later order—

More cyclical. Finite. Insistent.

LEFT COAST TRIPTYCH

1.
In a dusk of lavenders,
the crescent
of an incomplete overpass
on three dark pillars
of concrete.
The space between

admits the sintered lights
of Los Angeles,
cataclysmic downtown.
This could become
our Stonehenge,
a future ruin

as mute or fertile
as the pieces of Rome.
Gigantic ornament,
brocade of belts,
the interweaving
cloverleaves.

2.
No ramparts.
Just the transverse ranges
and coastal cliffs.
No stone chateaux
to predate remnants
of clay presidios.

What possible
likeness in Venice?
Abandoned canals
fraught with light
below the streets'
white noise.

Lone obelisk
of a graffiti'd lamppost.
And long monuments
in rock-bed, shifting
like the fictions
that claim us.

3.
We rest in the shade
of imported flora.
The sky is a speechless,
sun-struck god
and all our languages
to praise it are foreign.

The angels' city
overflows into valleys
named for saints.
A renaissance novel
promised griffins
and gold: an island

to the right hand
of the Indies,
where a Queen Califía
sang to her tribes
before horses,
highways, or mines.

BOUGAINVILLEA

Three true flowers and three bright bracts,
gaiety itself, the shrubby vine

soaring past its lattice
on a concrete wall above dirt

and loose stone, a path
to who knows where or what

but here—
an untended flourishing

astounds the casual
passer-by, who passes

swallows and cypresses
and shadows bent

with ease, up and
over the curves

of unremembered things.

OLIVES

Out among the felled limbs
of my in-laws' orchard
in the calm of winter,

I couldn't know
what would happen.
If there would ever be

another pregnancy.
Just that I needed
to step through tall grass

and feel the arc
of my boot-fall, the drop
of each olive

young or ripe—
apple green, old blood—
into the bucket.

Sun shifted.
Branch piles burned
at the grove's edge

and I gleaned, one
by one, perfect fruits.
Bucket to sack, sack to flatbed.

The muddy road
out to others
and commerce with others.

CANDLE LIGHTING

these candles waste fast
packed in the small

menorah I bought
last-minute they melt

each other as they burn
spilling themselves

toward the shallow cups
at the end of each

carved arm this religion
is full of cups and

candles and candles
in cups the turquoise

metal of Kiddush
Sabbath opening

with two pale arms
and closing with a braid

and a spice box
there are candles to light

weekly and yearly
and now because

we've lost one woman
who made a *yahrzeit*

for her husband we
close the year with two

in succession the white
glassed candles my father

places on a sill small rims
that glow above

the flame for one
night one day reflected

on the pane moved
by our passage

in the room by
our breath above them

OFFERING

This day. This hour.
Feast of paradox,

of plentitude
in the face of how
we are taught.

Scarcity, its army
of thoughts

feeding at the seed ball
now and off again

like the junco
or the house finch
red crest and all.

California Pantoum

Outside the school
mustard flanks the chain link,
cool fire of poppies
down the grass to the concrete curb.

Mustard flanks the chain link.
The smell of cheap pine, still green,
down the grass to the concrete curb,
and the odor of tar.

The smell of cheap pine, still green,
at the birthsite of tract homes,
and the odor of tar
from unfinished houses.

At the birthsite of tract homes
children play on sheetrock
from unfinished houses.
A shard of roof tile

where children play on sheetrock:
they know nothing of the echo
of a shard of roof tile
that rings of Barcelona,

they know nothing of the echo
of a cool fire of poppies
that rings of Barcelona
outside the school.

NEW YEAR'S DAY, COAST RANGE

Digging wild rose roots, shovel and pick,
we loosen earth around a young fig tree,
prepare a garden bed in the untamed space

between Alpine Road and a casual
apple grove, by scattered iris bulbs
and networks of blackberry. From this land

and its few wooden structures—a house,
tool shed and barn—we can see the blue slab
that extends from Pescadero, the cool

Pacific above elephant slopes
as the coast range shudders its first green.
Thin grass among ash thistle stalks. A ridge

slanting down to buckeye, greasewood
and fir; to the shaded base of a summit
wound with offshoots of the valley behind it,

wet roads where yesterday we saw
great plumed pockets of fog like white flame
rise from ravines that channel fire or rain.

First Rain

From April on, a marathon to mid-autumn.
Clouds shower nothing but light. Most days,
though, are cloudless. Faces of blank hills

shine like medallions, scallop the monotone blue.
By summer the peaks disappear into the wide
white haze that accumulates in valleys:

Santa Clara, San Fernando, San Joaquin,
incantations in the still air of noon.
Sun-baked stucco, a tide of traffic pressed

on soft asphalt. All day the locked cars swell
in parking lots furrowed by standing heat.
No wind carries eucalyptus fumes or the full

oleander shot with pink, flushed as though
fair-skinned. The concrete curbsides
lighten like clay, while loose-shirted tourists

wander Franciscan missions, fill pergolas,
pause in archways by tiled fountains
where the pigeons' grey sheens bob like clock-

work as they drink. Sweet shade of citrus
and grand jacarandas. Gardens where aloes abut
the rose the way neighborhoods abut the brush

along foothills and fluted canyons.
The first rain comes without temperance,
scattering dust with hard drops and raising

oil in suds. It answers the inland farms
along the interstate, their thousand white quills
of sprinklers on fields of green,

the prayers of grasslands for run-off,
of reservoirs for months of showers and a sky
retold in miles of open aqueduct.

II. KINGDOM OF SECRETS

THE SATELLITE SKY

As we dine the satellites spin.
We work and sleep, they pass the rim
of a village blank with snow.

Everywhere the day unfolds.
A monkey flinches in the banyan limbs
at the lip of a southern continent;

a missile stack, the storm-eye's path,
beneath the woven sky of satellites—
several hundred artificial sisters

to the moon. Their turning drums,
petals splayed, antennae like radiant
stamens. The bulbous roots of others

pace along their gentle arcs, relay
a voice in numbers, return to us the likes
of forestation, sea ice, smoke;

the good people of one country
indistinguishable from the next; my metal
desk a drop in the metropolis.

The great birds glide in their orbits,
fan themselves, jeweled heads humming
in a stream of signals. What moves

at the center of their gas hearts, delicate
as a pistil? They are the Ptolemaic angels
of the age. Deities simple as stars.

Beneath the lenses of their tempered eyes
a launch site slumbers, a combine rusts
in a field of weeds I entered in a dream,

knowing if I brought my words
to the marsh at its far edge, still
I could tell no one, not even the reeds.

FROM THE OFFICE OF GOVERNMENT SECURITY

I.
How do we secure?
Which walls, strictures?

A simple room and simple admonitions.

I signed my name
and I signed my name.
In the absence of windows.

Where fiction
is strictly prohibited
and words off limits, cut off.

Locked boxes of plain
English, even.

Plain English.

II.
He made small incisions in my document.
And I stood by like an anxious parent,
hands folded, questioning but silent
as a flurry of forbidden words flew out.

III.
Beside flesh-tone metal walls
and square-edged corrugated flanks
whose skirt weaves gravel and asphalt,

a wisteria blooms

unfettered and unchecked
along the lacey, beveled trough
of a barbed wire fence top.

CLEANROOM

Do not shed
your DNA here.

Restrain your hair.

Let no exhalation
fog or mist the air.

This jumpsuit, these
tissue boots
will rein you in

as no other
fashion can

while the bouffant cap,
in blue or white,
is the great

equalizer, making
grannies of all
as we tend

the sensitive
but tensile strong

that by dust specks
come undone.

SPACE

My father brought home
the blue-jacketed,

government-issued
views of the surface

of the moon. Parsed,
printed, and bearing

the crosshairs of our optics
on mottled fields

where illusion made
bubbles of craters

as we watched; my small
body tracking

toward a moon-cycle
still years away. Toward

wings I would seek
to merit, and a paper

to confirm my degree
in postulating the deep

workings of a universe
but not the world

who sings to us first, before
the logic of reason.

Before speech. Equations
forged in the engines

of memory. Hot interiors
of moments that meld

thought to muscle,
and words to thought.

BIOGRAPHY FILE

Your past, flat on the table
and dull as tin, can be pruned
beyond belief. Even in the concrete

there are excess facts: a street
lined with sycamore,
your mother's hair, the diary

of your adolescence
can all be omitted.
Give me certificates,

dates and degrees, professional
affiliations. There are figures,
and folders like mouths

to fill, lists of faces.
I am voracious for the set
type, the paraphrase, the one

title that will send you ripe
for filing, in drawers
with innumerable divisions.

MIDAS'S BARBER

Impossible to go on as before.

To un-know.

The king has sworn me to silence:

I've seen what is hidden
in his Phrygian cap.

What is left, then—

To speak freely in exile?
To sing like Pan?

Or turn my words
inward, into

the earth, bed of the
wind-swept rushes.

FLIGHT

1. Industry

In a kingdom of secrets, I crossed a shaded gap
between the guard booth and fields of asphalt
whose bed was tidal marsh. Structures rooted there.
Sunlight glared from windshields, from windowless skins
of buildings it did not penetrate. Thresholds took hold
along their flanks and numbered, unadorned façades.
Even debriefed and defrocked, I remain in their charge.
I handed the facts of my past to Security, my speech
to invisible partitions. Ciphers and rituals called me
through brash machine shops to a labyrinth
of cubicles; from sealed foyers into the bays of tall
hushed caverns, where nascent craft unfurled, pristine
in sulfur light. Extreme as the chaste white clusters
of dish antennas in bloom above barred gates.
Above gravel pathways where I could not escape
the scrutiny of sameness, or the fences laced
with barbs I took for runes of an unspoken order.

2. Piece Parts

In my white coat, in the quiet space
between shifts, I wait for things.

Things to be assembled, things to be tested.
As specified. And every thing is very clean.

The bins gleam with hardware stacked like treats:
jam nuts, star washers, pan-head screws—

My father's workbench strewn with magic shapes.
The pterodactyl heads of wire clips, pliers

like fish jaws, silver pigtails from the lathe
in that garage of patient making, of model wings

hung from the rafters, of tins with skull-and-
crossbones and Latin names to master.

3. L e s s o n s

I was born an eldest son.
Before I could read
my apprenticeship began

in crafting, by machine
and by hand, the tools
of flight. Engines tended,

tuned like bells across
my father's workshop.
When I was ten we cut

the first long ribs
for his first real airplane.
By its completion I had

breasts and soft hips.
The fuselage wore fine spruce,
the wings fleshed out

over rods and spars
and they weighed on me.
I helped to rig them,

to stitch and smooth
a skin of faultless silk
as all around us

notes of solder and epoxy,
of lanolin and gasoline
infused our hair, our clothes,

and settled on the spines
of metal parts in bins.
I chose to follow him.

Flying the middle course.
Setting out. And fearing—
not the frailty of mechanisms,

but an old fear
of failing. Of everything
except the spectacle of Earth

above my head, and sky
below, inverted by
my own hand at the yoke.

4. N i g h t

In dreams I am
without machine.

No airfoil, stick,
rudder—

a different physics

buoys me
kicking past cloud-forms

into each

moment
each moment.

5. M e s s a g e

Deep inside the complex I follow my colleague
through guard posts and locked corridors, until
we reach a room for secure communications.

I bear my special badge and fledgling *need-
to-know*. He holds all the combinations
and when he presses the last slow door open

it matters little that he's well-meaning
and polite, this man my father's age.
I see the black phone. And the red. Then

a Teletype with our message coming through.
All of it as antiquated as the paper
goddess pinned to the wall, her firmament

of dry acoustic tiles. Of strung fluorescents
whose hum beats in our veins and whose blurred
reflection drifts in broad linoleum.

He tears the message from the platen. We leave
without speaking, determined to wear nothing
of her presence between us. Handmaid

of a fading era. Stuck there too long
thigh-high in some ocean, poised on the verge
of stepping from the foam and moving on.

6. A s s e m b l y

They are sleeping.
On beds of polished
tooling, in sheets
of Mylar and copper,
they sleep.
With rigid fittings.
With drills and dies
loaned by the tool
crib, they wait
for weld tips
and bonding agents.
For curing agents
and solvent baths;
gloved hands, masked
faces, and final
accoutrement
of fine wiring
in this cradle

of circuit boards
and solar panels:
the ultra-clean
unfinished innards
and exoskeletons
of spacecraft.

7. M a z e

I didn't find a monster at the core.
No sacrifice. No thread to lead me out.
But I imagined the bureaucrats and brass
had a darker purpose than the safety
of democracy. Inside the cubicles,
the bullpens, the long bare halls with portals
to clock our every crossing, a unity
was lost on me. Much spoken of, but missing.

8. P o l y g r a p h

What are they sampling,
these slender antennae

whose clubbed tips
startle and drift

over paper tape?
Which truths

do they taste,
how many

evade
the thin dark

sap they weep?

9. Briefing

Once my kindergarten teacher ordered silence.
I couldn't ask permission for the girls' room

and walked home wet, down to the lace cuffs
of my ankle socks. Already someone had

started to slip. Taking leave of her clear voice,
going under. By twenty, well forgotten.

Until I faltered, heavy-legged, heading down
an empty hall. No comforts, not even a bench

for waiting out whatever gives you pause
when things appear exactly as they should.

And I see myself enter that office. Its lack
of windows, its wood-like meeting table,

where we receive the ways of coded work.
The briefer, who reads aloud from a big book.

Her plastic picture-badge, her sensible dress
and hair. There will be words to lock away

before we are dismissed, and others to commit
to heart. Questions flutter at the base of my throat.

But the book has closed. Agreements are dispersed.
On every sheet, I make the shapes that mean

my name, in ordinary ink, and a precipice
gives way. Too distant to hear—skeins of roots

and clotted soil, the cleaving soft ledge, lost
foothold—all sinking, to lodge beneath

the stuff of dreams: a woman crouched
in a tree, hair unkempt, not articulate.

10. Laboratory

Three flights
up to the ladies'
room.

Cracked paint.
Basement labs
where my data

gather, a smattering
of electrons
in a vacuum chamber.

My grandfather built optics here.

My father followed
in a crew cut,
white shirt, narrow tie.

In snapshots
and clippings I see
men smile.

The hard
truth shines—

Pioneer, Ranger, Mariner.
Aluminum soldiers.
Unswerving.

Years later he
tells me one

flew into the sun.

11. Refuge

At the tidal edge I touch razor wire
and rusting barbs, and see the wintering
geese alight from one side to the other;
preening, feeding, noting our presence through
the open weave of the fence. The hiking trail
meets the refuge at a common boundary:
a selvage of metal. With a view over
marsh and fennel, mudflats pocked by egrets.
From here, the labyrinth assumes the hues
of any business park along the bay.
Its outermost buildings supplanted, remade;
its core the steady keeper of signatures,
if not the hands who fabricated those
fantastic birds, observers of us all.

12. Sighting

Is one of those lights, caught for an instant
between stars, our handiwork
flashing back at us through the space
of decades?

In flight at last, or rather falling,
over and over, into its orbit
of ice and fire, visible now
through night's invisible atmosphere.

III. MODELS

ARCHAEOPTERYX

Perfect as Nike.

Head bent, feathers
arrested.

The imprint
of upturned wings
a likeness

to wonder at——
your last

flight, dear prototype.

To the Makers

I want to tell them, all of them, the living
and the dead. Not about gratitude. I want
them to know. To tell them that it happens,
years or ages after their labors. It happens
with their work in my hand, on a bowed page,
at or near the end of a phrase. A fissure
opens onto the deep lake of their making,
its slate skin and forested rim. Tools strewn
on the silty bottom: wavering shapes, soft
with life along grooves and shanks. Through this
water, through murk and sun-shaft and clear shoals,
the pressure building or falling off, they dove
and rose, time and again. Hauling, gleaning,
and leaving the lake, to make a portal from words.

BLACKBOARD

after the watercolor by Winslow Homer

She is at the blackboard, a young woman
with one arm behind her waist. Her other hand
tilts a wooden pointer when she pauses,
placid as the markings meant for an unseen
class to master: parallel lines, a right
angle, an equilateral triangle.

Her apron is a sea of blue-and-white check,
her dress awash with the gray of the wainscot
where chalk floats on a narrow tray.
Her hem breaks onto a floor the color
of flattened sand. The shell of one black shoe
protrudes and completes the equilibrium.

She may stand this way forever: brow tangent
to a circle the size of her head. Turned hip
and canted shoulder. A profile of measured
resolve, that says her thoughts are not tucked
beneath the ivory ribbon, but directed
where her eyes rest, at some point not in the room.

The Big White Dress

I will sew you a self
of moon-cloth,
color of angels

and aristocracy.
The shape will buoy you
till your head is an icon,

your hands twin flame
above the weeping guests.
What are nebulae

to this radiance?
The big white dress
floats up it knows

the clouds are its
correspondence,
the sky its bed.

I let it go,
work of a hundred hands
from a hundred ages.

Draping and tatting,
forbidden stitch,
the eyes made dim by it,

our spines bent
over lace, a thread loop,
such frailty—

like a huge bell of chalk,
made only to marvel at.
All that we know is beaded

in clusters and strung
on the spidery lines
between motifs,

and we ask nothing.
We do not ask
for the blood-spot,

for innocence blind
as a sheet, for shy
obeisance.

The linen is
laid for your path,
sheer as a blaze.

The dress incarnates a day,
the day we are trained for.
There is a song

at the end of it,
there is ascension.
Even your hair

will flower
and your pupils reflect
the mass of corollas you clasp.

KWIKSILVER

Four years old, I pose with a model airplane
on the front lawn. It is bigger than I am.
Nosewheel and wingtip lean into the grass
beside the transmitter, the one with a beetle-
green metal housing, long obsolete.
I kneel, holding the neck of the Kwiksilver
against my shoulder, not seeing all
I am modeling on a morning of open sky.
In a moment's breadth. In flagrant light.

EMILY

I am looking for a word, and there she is
in her capped sleeves and ribbon choker,
hair back in a bun. She holds a wrapped sprig
of something bright, all in the sharp oval
on the margin of a page: her surname fixed
in the span from *dichotomy* to *didn't*,
four entries past a novelist whose works
were not tied in bundles in the family home,
but set to print within his lifetime—and hers.
Maker of gardens, music, bread, and poems;
witness to sorrows in a phrase of light
we can listen for again. And I almost
didn't. I heard the failings of her time
from inside the dichotomies of mine.

MARINER 10

Late afternoon, clearing
a bookshelf or closet, we enter
the unrecorded inventory
of what enters our lives:
dusted off, smaller than we
remember. Or scaled down.

These bright facets
of sheet aluminum,
the photo reproductions
of solar panels, lathed
hinges on which they splay
open to the same sun

their namesake journeyed toward
when my grandfather, who built
both namesake and model,
worked the curved surfaces
of mirror and lens
in a laboratory on a hill.

*

Wingèd octagon, unmanned,
unpersonned. Messenger
to the messenger planet.
Humble cartographer
of spheres. Asleep now, lost
to us, circling the sun.

*

With a seventh-grade schooling, he learned
by ingenuity. Gleaning from models
what he lacked in math, crafting
mockups, he found the fit of each design
and honed its elements in keeping with
the laws of light as they spoke through him.

*

Dear Harold, when I read the plaques
and commendations, I do not remember
your raw brilliance, but rather a silver lunch-
box and thermos, your zippered cloth jacket.
The back steps of the small kitchen
where you returned from the Lab
to the metal-scented, soft cacophony
of ham radio on your desk at home.

*

Models, plaques, and photographs.
The past in orbit around us.

MOON JELLIES

Animate
in the back-lit
black tank

you fly——

lace-edged
ghost bells,

propelled
by such grace
as I cannot

match with my
clumsy spine,
my

opacity,

the aging truths
inside me unseen

and unborn,
stung
by the fact of your

eggs in arced rows:

hot flower
in a clear skull.

MATISSE ON SILICON

A seated nude instead of circuitry:
bare silver pools of torso, head, and limb
afloat in blue. Wafer as estuary,

where business flows into the salt of calm
insouciance, of sex, and doesn't smile.
There's proof of what this wafer could have been,

microscopic features shot in profile:
crenellations and tapered phalluses.
Matisse's nude is on a grander scale

plain to the naked eye. She displaces
the stuff of livelihoods, your own perhaps—
row upon row laid down for devices

with tracery more intricate than stained glass
and equally solemn. This trade prefers
silicon wrought by hot metals in gas,

a palette fine as any Old Master's,
suited to experiment and polished craft,
and reinvention if the work endures.

A Bavarian Sofa

It came here bare,
an eighteenth-century skeleton.

More like sculpture—

the crest rail worn by erasures,
matching cherubim,
griffins, fleurs-de-lis.

Desire
for the scraped gold-leaf.
The claw feet. The freight

of empire.
A manageable piece.

GLOBE

The Earth on an axis of brass, tilted back,
spun for the fun of it. For the contrast
of mountains and seas under our fingertips;
for the pastel blur of states whose names will slip

out of usage. As if a typeface could
fix them, or their old grievances find peace
in polygons. We know the globe will yield
some day to the next great framing of space;

will rest in its mesh of meridians
beside the hard-bound lexicon, laid open,
inviting us to navigate between

a grace shared with the crudest of stone tools,
and the gravity of models and names
we hold above revision, and fear to lose.

THE AEROBAT

High on his shoulder, my father holds
one of his progeny for the world to see.
The Los Angeles sky is an almost
forgotten blue above his quiet smile,
and he is far younger than I am now.

The cowling glints. The propeller, spotless,
installed for the snapshot, no doubt. I can feel
the odd empty heft of balsa, the sandy finish
of dope on taut wing skin, through which the ribs
are visible at a distance greater than years.

O weekend days of wood parts drying
on waxed paper at the kitchen table, my mother
worried over glue fumes and X-Acto blades
as engines cured in the oven, as engines
bathed in our garage and solder smoked

beside an ashtray. The workbench teeming,
tools and piece parts a rambling terrain
anchored by a rounded steel vise. Pushrods
and plywood. Spinners and pins. Plans or
boxed kits, for models fashioned with deference

as his questions took root. As he ventured,
slide rule in hand, to draft the Aerobat;
to meet what years of practice and delight
had seeded in him. And this is how we land.
Forging our own craft, and finding origin.

A DIFFERENT PHYSICS

To meet the world with a different physics than the one
we built our lives on. To free a body of notation—

each set of laws more fundamental than the last
attempt: a wry music, a supple net to cast

onto the sea of meaning. There's a physics outside
the blackboard's edge, and one we seek to unify,

grandly, in our time or next time, maybe. Next time
around we might articulate more with less, and roam

the spacious box of bigger thought, to find ourselves
at ease in the seeking, and the not-seeking. No cause

but joy in both, with a single word for *a-thing-
and-its-opposite* finally at home on our tongue.

LEPIDOPTERA

Minute lights of white wings flitting
through shafts of sun between trees.

*

Spread wings:

a ravished
bivalve
crusted with mud.

Rough symmetries
long after

the gull's feast.

*

A shower, a flurrying out
from the maple's canopy—
wings turned wingèd
seed pods in my hand.

*

I've wanted this.
A liquid transition.
The clarity before
and after.

An eye like a thousand
dew drops

sees the fount
of nectar

and lands there.

SPACE 2

There is nowhere to go because we are
already here, our sphere among others,
our egg-shaped path around the sun, in space
we name *the sky*. It's all sky above our feet,
between us; carrying the weight of myth
and breath, the towhee's metal call at dawn,
my child's call through the fragile din that is
the world knowing itself, and not knowing.

The moon lived as a flat, if lovely, disk,
until the afternoon that I watched pass
across the sun a black yolk. A body.
Then, all the sky bodies I could not see
changed at once, together, freed of my mind's eye,
into the shapes that they had always known.

My *Kouros*

Even his penis was serene.
His bearded grin, a beacon,
drew me in.

I kept going back to him.

In the Louvre
I lingered
by the many moons of his face,

the marmoreal torsos
glassed in—

he couldn't step
despite the gesture.
And that Archaic smile was all a sham.

Un-fist the hands.

Unmake him.

My warrior, athlete,
fragment horseman:

I unmake him
down to the face
of my young self

taking everything in
without lover
or guardian.

Stone flakes. Pedestal. Set pin.
Not the ruins of a life

but a casting.

HEART OF AUTUMN

Is it always this elemental? Boulder, reeds,
and water. Thoughts skimming off the pond
to meet you. And geese flapping
near the far shore. A wood platform
toward the center, past three blue buoys
demarcating the shallows from the depths
like seasons, like intent from invitation.

'ZERO DEFECTS'

I want a new
notion of perfection.

One to live with

in my defect-full
humanness—

bone-cache,
chatter and

thought-breast.
Let me admit

the whole
within the scrap

and learn to hold
scrappiness
on a par

with truth.
As truth moves

to plural. As we
fail and flourish

beyond
the slashed zero.

VITRUVIAN CHILD

Vitruvian child, with your arms flung wide,
your bare feet riding that faithful circle
day into night, day upon age upon eon—

Reach for my hand, out beyond the box-tips
where your fingers stretch toward eternity,
where your likenesses thrive untethered

to provinces of gender, to purviews
of paper and ink. Tell me how harmonies
swirl from the famous shapes that frame you,

how your many selves dwell in that flowering
of limbs. Show us what freedoms you've devised,
how an open frame becomes a plaything

through every season, and in every light.

"Introduction to Methods of Mathematical Physics" takes its title from Physics 104 at the University of California at Davis.

"Perseverance" began in response to *Rattle* magazine's ekphrastic challenge, which featured the collage *Metamorphosis 2* by Thomas Terceira.

"Bull Thistle" is for Rieneke Zessoules and in memory of Añole Dahlstrom.

"Night Fire" draws on Elizabeth Bishop's poem "Night City."

"Left Coast Triptych" touches on unsettled histories of California's naming.

"New Year's Day, Coast Range" is for Martha Kimball, John Nurre, and David Putnam.

The title "Cleanroom" is also the term for a controlled environment, used in research and manufacturing, that is free from specified levels of dust and other airborne contaminants.

"Kwiksilver" and "The Aerobat" are titled for radio-controlled model airplanes designed by my father, Larry Rosenberg. These models appeared respectively in the November 1966 and February 1969 issues of *R/C Modeler Magazine* and were later sold online. "The Aerobat" is for my mother, Sandra Rosenberg, and my siblings, Erika and Greg.

"Mariner 10" remembers my paternal grandfather, Harold H. Rosenberg, who worked at the Jet Propulsion Laboratory from the 1960s to the mid-1970s. With no formal schooling beyond age thirteen, he was hired based on an exam and was later awarded an honorary engineering degree. He was instrumental in developing the first lunar cameras. I thank my extended family for detailed recollections of this history.

"Matisse on Silicon" refers to silicon wafers on which semiconductor devices, such as microchips, are made. My friend Ines Morales made the uncanny selection of Matisse's *Blue Nude II* for the wafer she patterned in a device processing class.

"Space 2" was written following the annular eclipse of 2012. I am grateful to the Plamondon-Matheny family for the viewing party and eye gear.

"'Zero Defects'" gets its title from the name of a pivotal manufacturing quality management program developed in the US aerospace and defense sectors during the 1960s. It became a trade slogan and was adopted worldwide in other industries.

Acknowledgements

I have been blessed with extraordinary colleagues, teachers, mentors, family, and friends. That list has grown considerably during the long process of finding a home for this collection. I am tremendously grateful to all of you for fostering my work in many contexts.

It has been my great fortune to study with gifted teachers. Eavan Boland, Olga Broumas, Simone Di Piero, Ken Fields, Sandra M. Gilbert, Jeff Haller, Shihan Robert Nadeau, Robert Pinsky, Alan Shapiro, Alan Soldofsky, Rosanna Warren, and, in memoriam, Celia Millward and Derek Walcott: Thank you for helping me find each new territory of learning. I am deeply thankful for those who support the transformative Wallace Stegner Fellowship at Stanford University. Gratitude to my physics cohort at the University of California at Davis, fellow writers at Boston University, and the extended family of Stegner Fellows. My writers' group of the past ten years is an ongoing source of creative community: Nancy Etchemendy, Narada Hess, Rick Mamelock, MaryLee McNeal, Nancy Mohr, Marian Slattery, and Ward Trueblood. For editorial insight I thank Talila Baron, Bryn Garrehy, Jeffrey Harrison, Rick Hilles, and Erika Rosenberg. To Nan Cohen, Gage McKinney, and Kim Van Tran, I give my profound gratitude for longtime friendship and your role in shaping many of these poems. Thank you: Ann Badillo, Janis and Jordan Bajor, Ted Jenvey, and Cindy Winslow. My thanks to friends in aviation, and colleagues in engineering and consulting for your camaraderie, support, and our shared endeavors.

I wish to thank as well as commend the San Mateo County Board of Supervisors for creating, under the guidance of Supervisor Warren Slocum and Supervisor Carole Groom, the Poet Laureate position; and my friend and predecessor, Caroline Goodwin, for her stellar foundational work. The laureate appointment has afforded more doors and minds open to poetry than I would otherwise encounter in daily life.

Red Mountain Press and judge Irena Praitis astonished me with their swift welcome of the manuscript. My thanks to Devon Ross, to Susan Gardner for her generosity and instructive editing, and to Irena for her gracious, nuanced reception of this work.

My family has mentored me in more ways than I can articulate. My mother, Sandra, is a source of unwavering love and encouragement. My gratitude every day to Maki and Zoé: Your love, wisdom, and humor sustain me.

I hold in loving memory family, friends, and mentors who guide me still, and these dear model-mentors: my maternal grandmother, Pauline Lewis Saltman, and my father. Pauline, this book is yours. Larry, I've finally built my airplane.